GRAPHIC DINOSAURS

OVIRAPTOR

THE EGG THIEF

BY ROB SHONE

PowerKiDS press

New York

Published in 2012 by The Rosen Publishing Group, Inc.
29 East 21st Street, New York, NY 10010

Designed and produced by
David West Books

Designed and written by Rob Shone

Photographic credits: 5ml, Beatrice Murch; 5m, Zoharby; 5br, Manfrad Werner (GNU-FDL); 30bl, Steve Starer; 30bm/br, Ryan Somer.

Library of Congress Cataloging-in-Publication Data
Shone, Rob.
Oviraptor : the egg thief / by Rob Shone.
p. cm. — (Graphic dinosaurs)
Includes index.
ISBN 978-1-4488-5207-9 (library binding) — ISBN 978-1-4488-5255-0 (pbk.)
— ISBN 978-1-4488-5256-7 (6-pack)
1. Oviraptor—Juvenile literature. I. Title. II. Series.
QE862.S3S453 2012
567.912—dc22
2011003216

Manufactured in China

CPSIA Compliance Information: Batch #DS1102PK:
For Further Information contact Rosen Publishing, New York, New York at 1-800-237-9932

CONTENTS

WHAT IS AN OVIRAPTOR?

OVIRAPTOR MEANS "EGG THIEF."

The horny crest on Oviraptor's head was hollow and filled with thin sheets of bone. It acted like an automobile's radiator, keeping the Oviraptor cool.

Oviraptors did not have teeth, but they did have two bony **prongs** *in the roof of their mouth. These were used to break open the hard shells of eggs, clams, and snails.*

Oviraptors had a beak rather than a snout. Strong jaw muscles gave them a powerful bite.

Although Oviraptors could not fly, they had feathers to keep them warm during cold desert nights.

Oviraptors' hands and claws were long and their wrists were very flexible, ideal for catching small lizards and mammals.

Oviraptors had long legs and were fast runners.

OVIRAPTOR WAS A DINOSAUR THAT LIVED AROUND 75 TO 65 MILLION YEARS AGO, DURING THE **CRETACEOUS PERIOD**. **FOSSILS** OF ITS SKELETON HAVE BEEN FOUND IN MONGOLIA AND CHINA.

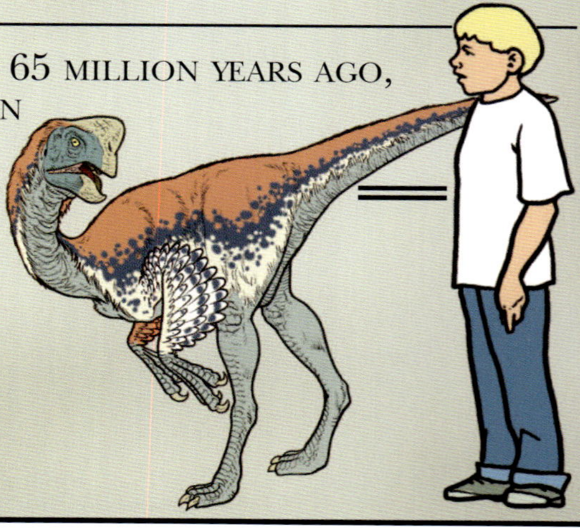

An adult Oviraptor measured up to 6 feet (1.8 m) long, stood 3 feet (0.9 m) high at the shoulder, and weighed 60 lbs (27 kg).

DINO-BIRDS

The Oviraptor family (called Oviraptorids) contained dinosaurs that were very bird like. All Oviraptorids had a toothless beak and feathers. One Oviraptorid, Nomingia, even had a special bone at the end of its tail called a pygostyle. This is the bone to which birds' fan-shaped tail feathers are attached.

Oviraptor had a powerful beak, just as parrots do today.

HEAD CRESTS

Almost every Oviraptorid had a horny crest on its head. Scientists believe that Oviraptor had one, even though the skull of the only Oviraptor fossil to exist is badly crushed. The crests were hollow and filled with paper-thin bones. The spaces between the bones were connected to the dinosaur's nostrils. The crests may have acted like automobile radiators and helped to keep the Oviraptors cool in the desert heat. They may also have been colored and used to identify individual dinosaurs.

DESERT DWELLERS

Oviraptors lived in what is now Mongolia's Gobi Desert. Conditions there today are very similar to those that existed 70 million years ago, when Oviraptors lived. Large areas of sand dunes and rocky desert were watered by streams, rivers, and oases, fed by seasonal rains.

Many new dinosaurs have been discovered in Mongolia's Gobi Desert (above).

Like Oviraptor, the Southeast Asian cassowary (right) has a horny crest. The flightless bird uses it to crash through the dense undergrowth of its jungle home.

PART ONE... THE GOOD MOTHER

THE NEST IS A SHALLOW BOWL JUST WIDE ENOUGH FOR THE OVIRAPTOR TO SIT IN. SHE STARTS TO LAY HER EGGS, TWO AT A TIME, IN A CIRCLE AROUND THE EDGE OF THE NEST.
AFTER A WEEK THE OVIRAPTOR STOPS LAYING. SHE HAS 14 EGGS TO CARE FOR.
THE MOTHER WILL SIT ON THE EGGS FOR MANY DAYS.

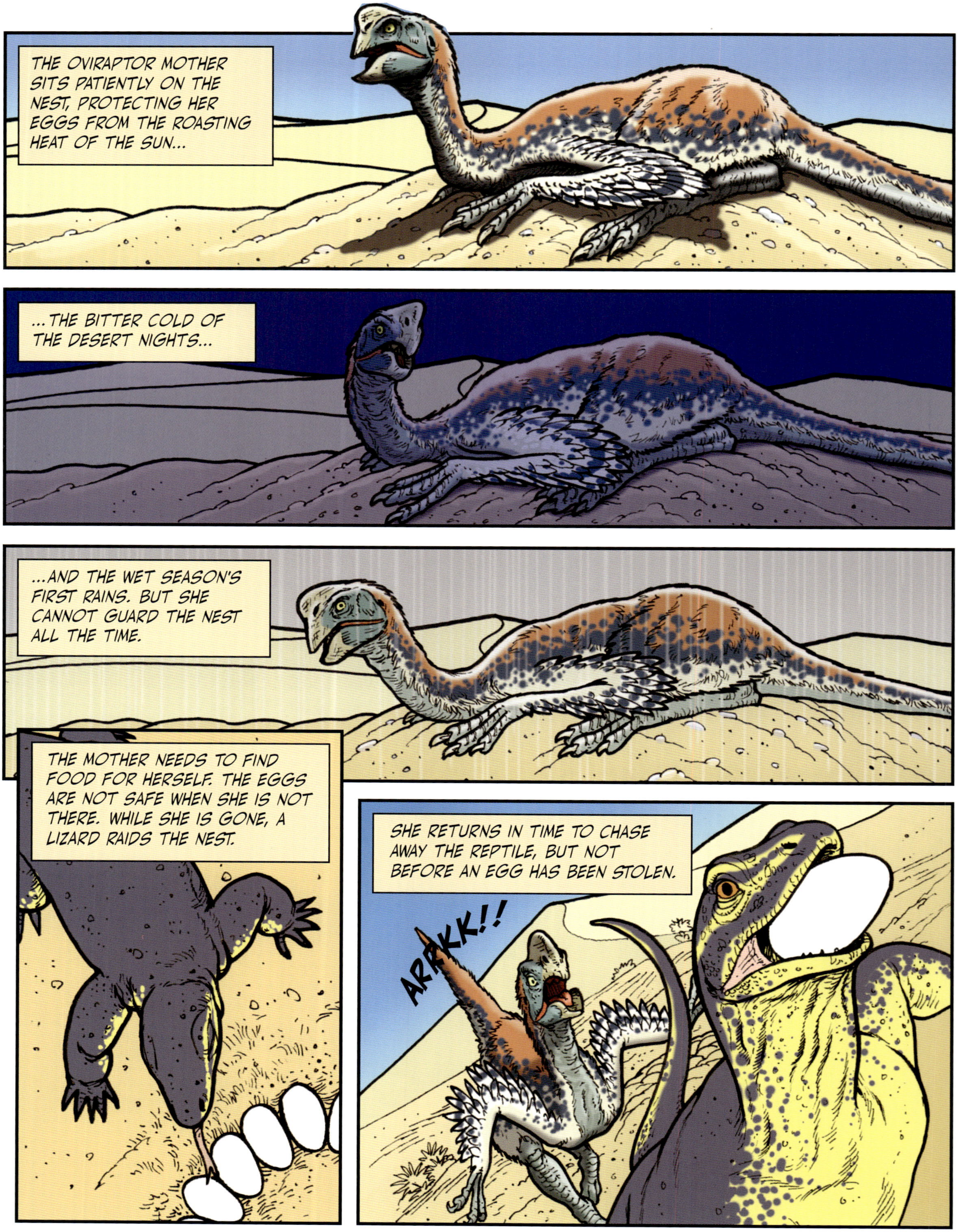
THE OVIRAPTOR MOTHER SITS PATIENTLY ON THE NEST, PROTECTING HER EGGS FROM THE ROASTING HEAT OF THE SUN...
...THE BITTER COLD OF THE DESERT NIGHTS...
...AND THE WET SEASON'S FIRST RAINS. BUT SHE CANNOT GUARD THE NEST ALL THE TIME.
THE MOTHER NEEDS TO FIND FOOD FOR HERSELF. THE EGGS ARE NOT SAFE WHEN SHE IS NOT THERE. WHILE SHE IS GONE, A LIZARD RAIDS THE NEST.
SHE RETURNS IN TIME TO CHASE AWAY THE REPTILE, BUT NOT BEFORE AN EGG HAS BEEN STOLEN.
ARRKK!!

SMALL LIZARDS ARE EASY ENOUGH FOR THE OVIRAPTOR TO DEAL WITH, BUT SHE HAS OTHER ENEMIES IN THE DESERT THAT ARE MUCH LARGER. A PACK OF VELOCIRAPTORS HAVE SEEN THE NESTING OVIRAPTOR. LIKE LIZARDS, THEY WILL EAT THE EGGS. THEY WILL NOT STOP THERE, THOUGH. THEY WILL ALSO EAT THE MOTHER.
THE MEAT EATERS MOVE TOWARD THE NEST.
THE OVIRAPTOR HAS SEEN THEM BUT DOES NOT RUN AWAY. SHE STANDS OVER HER EGGS, PROTECTING THEM FROM THE DANGER.
WARRKK!!
SZZAAHHRR!!
THE VELOCIRAPTORS STOP. THEY SENSE SOMETHING IS WRONG.

A DARK SHAPE APPEARS AT THE TOP OF THE DUNE OVERLOOKING THE NEST. IT IS A TARCHIA, A LARGE ARMORED DINOSAUR.
IT IS NOT ALONE. A WHOLE HERD OF TARCHIA ARE TRAVELING TO THE RIVER TO DRINK, AND THE NEST IS IN THEIR PATH.
THE VELOCIRAPTORS TURN AND RUN.

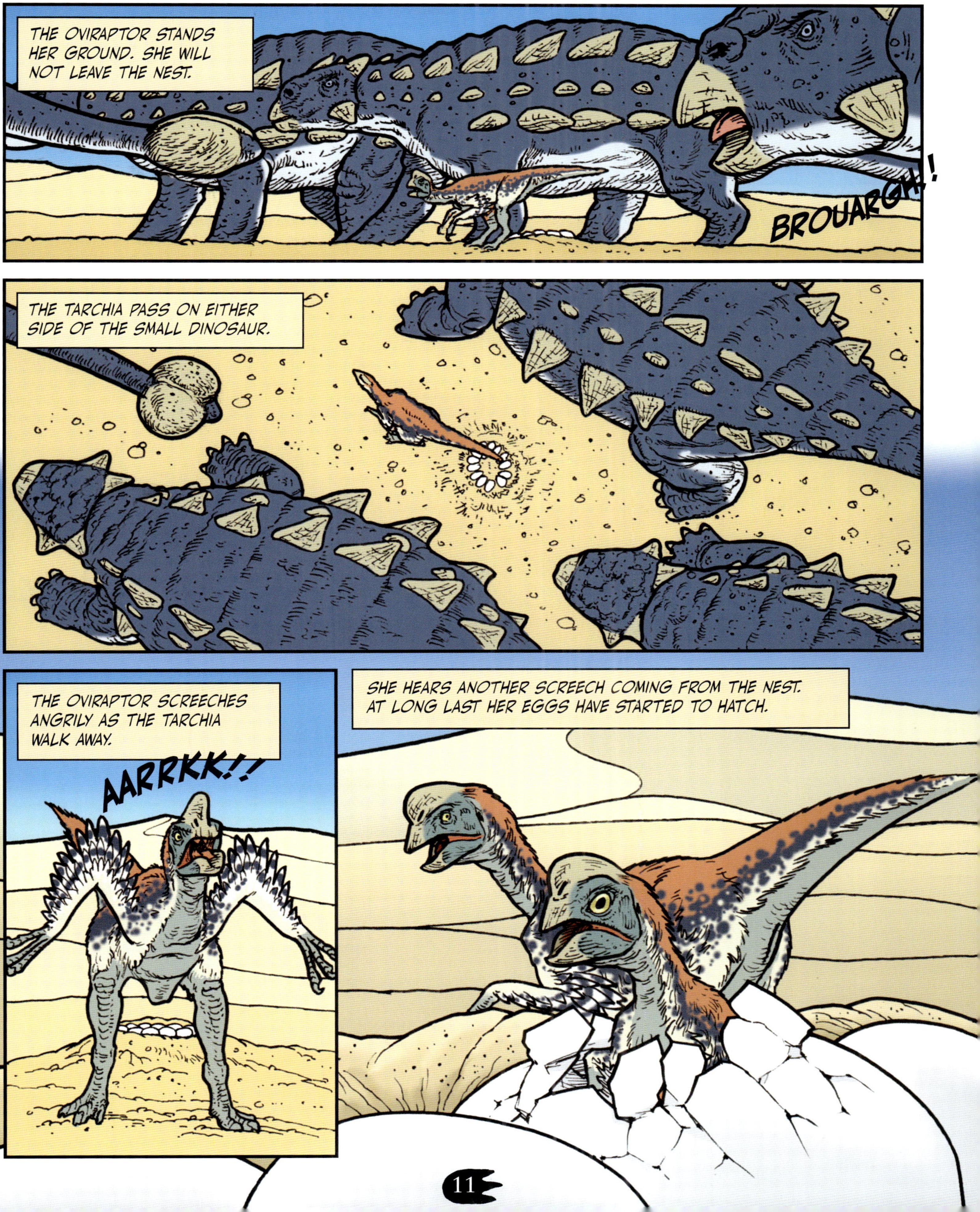
THE OVIRAPTOR STANDS HER GROUND. SHE WILL NOT LEAVE THE NEST.
BROUARGH!!
THE TARCHIA PASS ON EITHER SIDE OF THE SMALL DINOSAUR.
THE OVIRAPTOR SCREECHES ANGRILY AS THE TARCHIA WALK AWAY.
AARRKK!!
SHE HEARS ANOTHER SCREECH COMING FROM THE NEST. AT LONG LAST HER EGGS HAVE STARTED TO HATCH.

PART TWO... THE RIVERSIDE

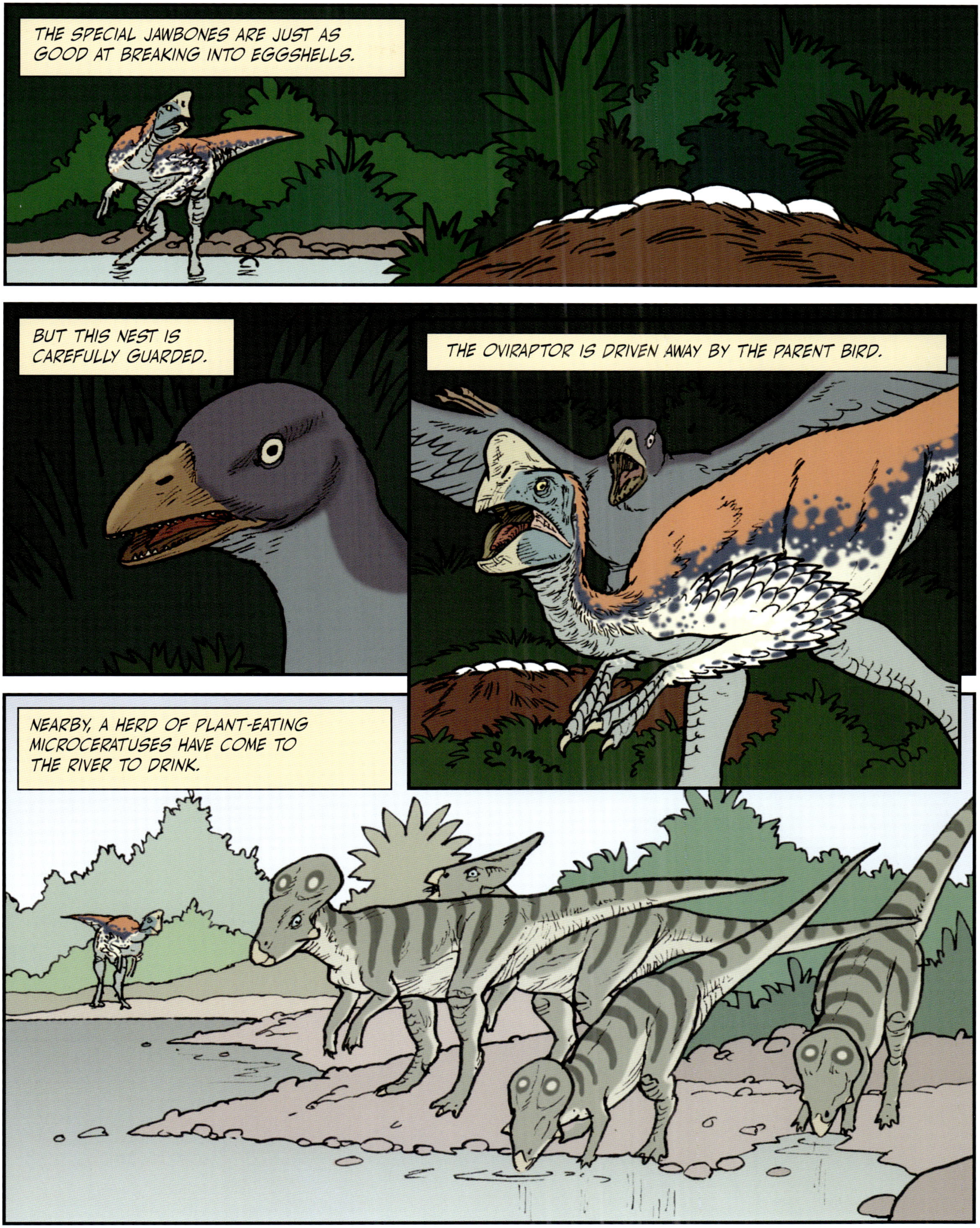
THE SPECIAL JAWBONES ARE JUST AS GOOD AT BREAKING INTO EGGSHELLS.
BUT THIS NEST IS CAREFULLY GUARDED.
THE OVIRAPTOR IS DRIVEN AWAY BY THE PARENT BIRD.
NEARBY, A HERD OF PLANT-EATING MICROCERATUSES HAVE COME TO THE RIVER TO DRINK.

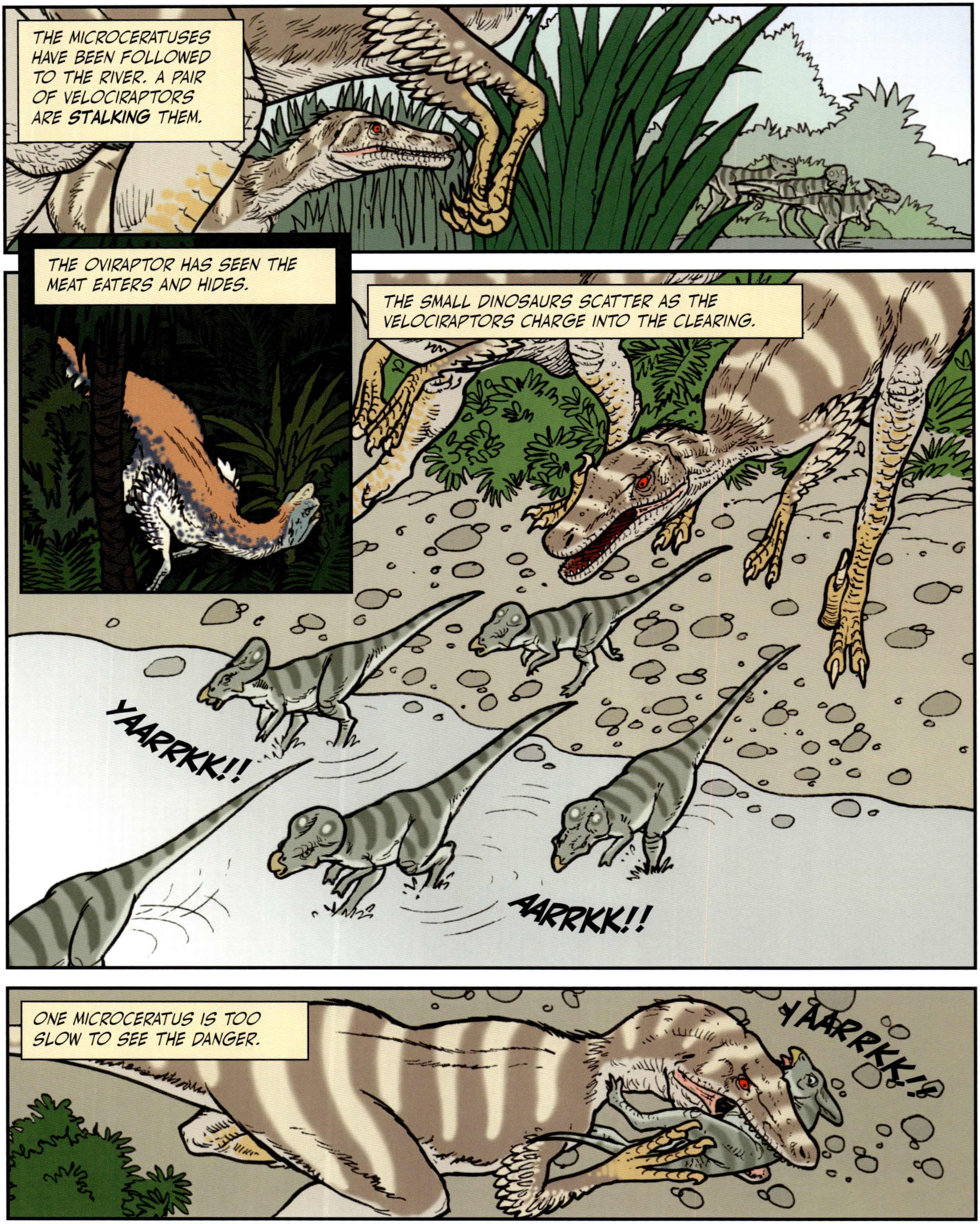
THE MICROCERATUSES HAVE BEEN FOLLOWED TO THE RIVER. A PAIR OF VELOCIRAPTORS ARE **STALKING** THEM.
THE OVIRAPTOR HAS SEEN THE MEAT EATERS AND HIDES.
THE SMALL DINOSAURS SCATTER AS THE VELOCIRAPTORS CHARGE INTO THE CLEARING.
YAARRKK!!
AARRKK!!
ONE MICROCERATUS IS TOO SLOW TO SEE THE DANGER.
YAARRKK!!

THE VELOCIRAPTOR DOES NOT GET TO ENJOY ITS KILL. A THERIZINOSAURUS WANDERS INTO THE CLEARING TO FEED, AND IT WANTS TO FEED ALONE. THE PLANT EATER WAVES ITS HUGE CLAWS, HALF AS LONG AS A VELOCIRAPTOR, AT THE MEAT EATERS.
RRAARRHHHGHH!!

THE VELOCIRAPTORS RUN, LEAVING THE DEAD MICROCERATUS BEHIND.

FROM HER HIDING PLACE THE OVIRAPTOR CAN SEE THE DEAD MICROCERATUS. OVIRAPTORS WILL EAT LIZARDS, MAMMALS, AND EVEN SMALL DINOSAURS IF THEY CAN CATCH THEM.

HERE IS A MEAL THAT DOES NOT NEED TO BE HUNTED.

BUT THE FEEDING DINOSAUR IS STANDING OVER THE MICROCERATUS'S BODY. SNATCHING IT FROM BENEATH THE THERIZINOSAURUS'S LARGE FEET WILL NOT BE EASY.

A CITIPATI, HIDDEN FROM SIGHT, HAS SEEN EVERYTHING. THE OVIRAPTOR'S LARGER RELATIVE ALSO WANTS THE FREE MEAL.
WHEN THE THERIZINOSAURUS MOVES AWAY FROM THE MICROCERATUS, THE OVIRAPTOR SEES HER CHANCE. SHE DARTS INTO THE CLEARING...
...AND GRABS IT.
AT THAT MOMENT THE CITIPATI BURSTS FROM THE FERNS AND RUSHES AT THE OVIRAPTOR.

THE OVIRAPTOR, WITH HER PRIZE IN HER JAWS, TURNS...
...AND RUNS.
THE CITIPATI FOLLOWS...
...SNAPPING AT THE OVIRAPTOR'S TAIL.

THE CITIPATI IS JUST ABOUT TO CATCH THE OVIRAPTOR, WHEN...
ZHARRGH!
...THE GROUND GIVES WAY BENEATH ITS FEET. THE CITIPATI HAS RUN INTO A MUDDY BOG.
THE OVIRAPTOR ESCAPES INTO THE UNDERGROWTH, LEAVING THE CITIPATI BEHIND, TRAPPED IN THE THICK, STICKY SLUDGE.
THE CITIPATI IS NOT ALONE FOR LONG.
SZNARRH!

PART THREE... THE VOLCANO

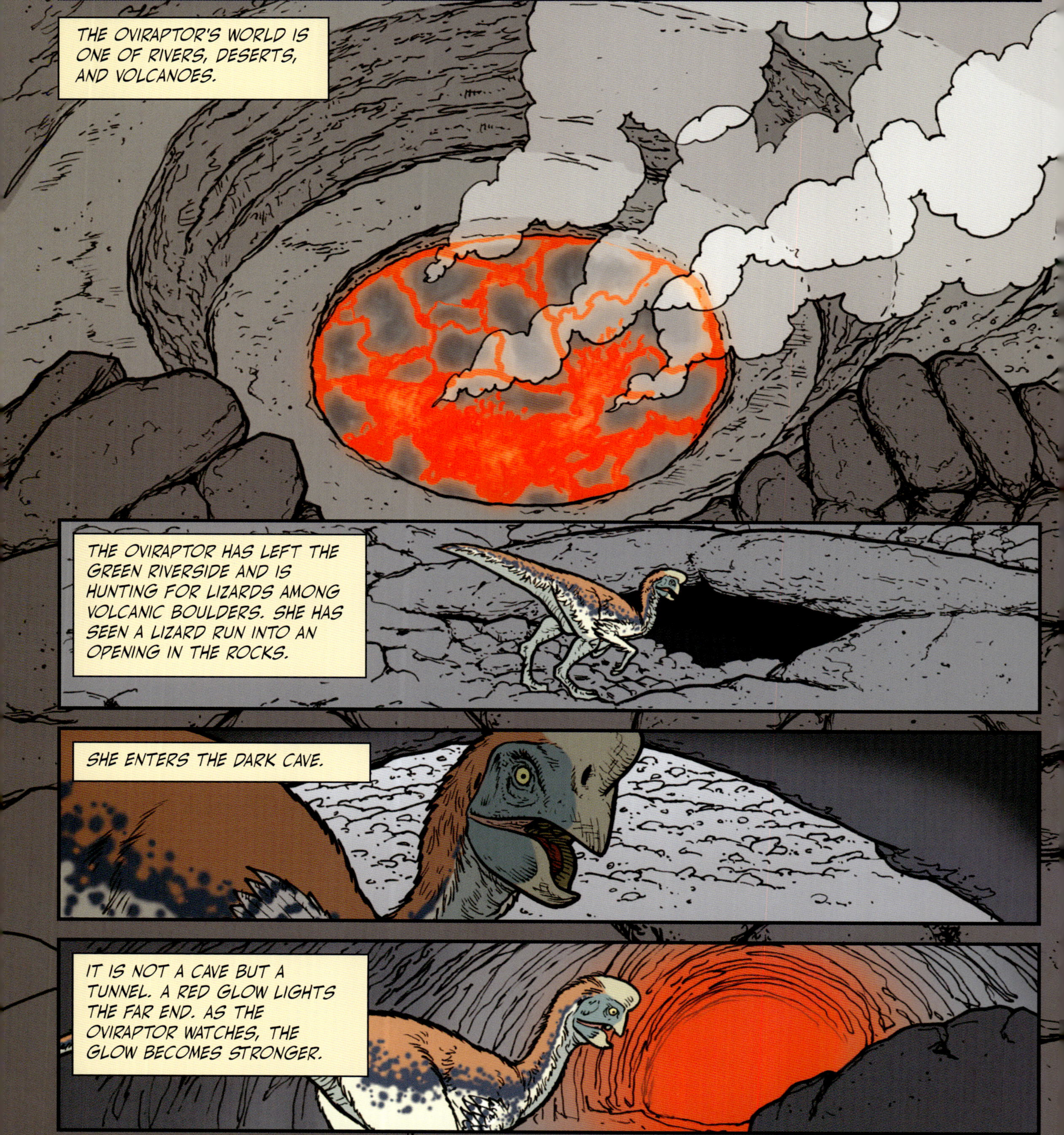

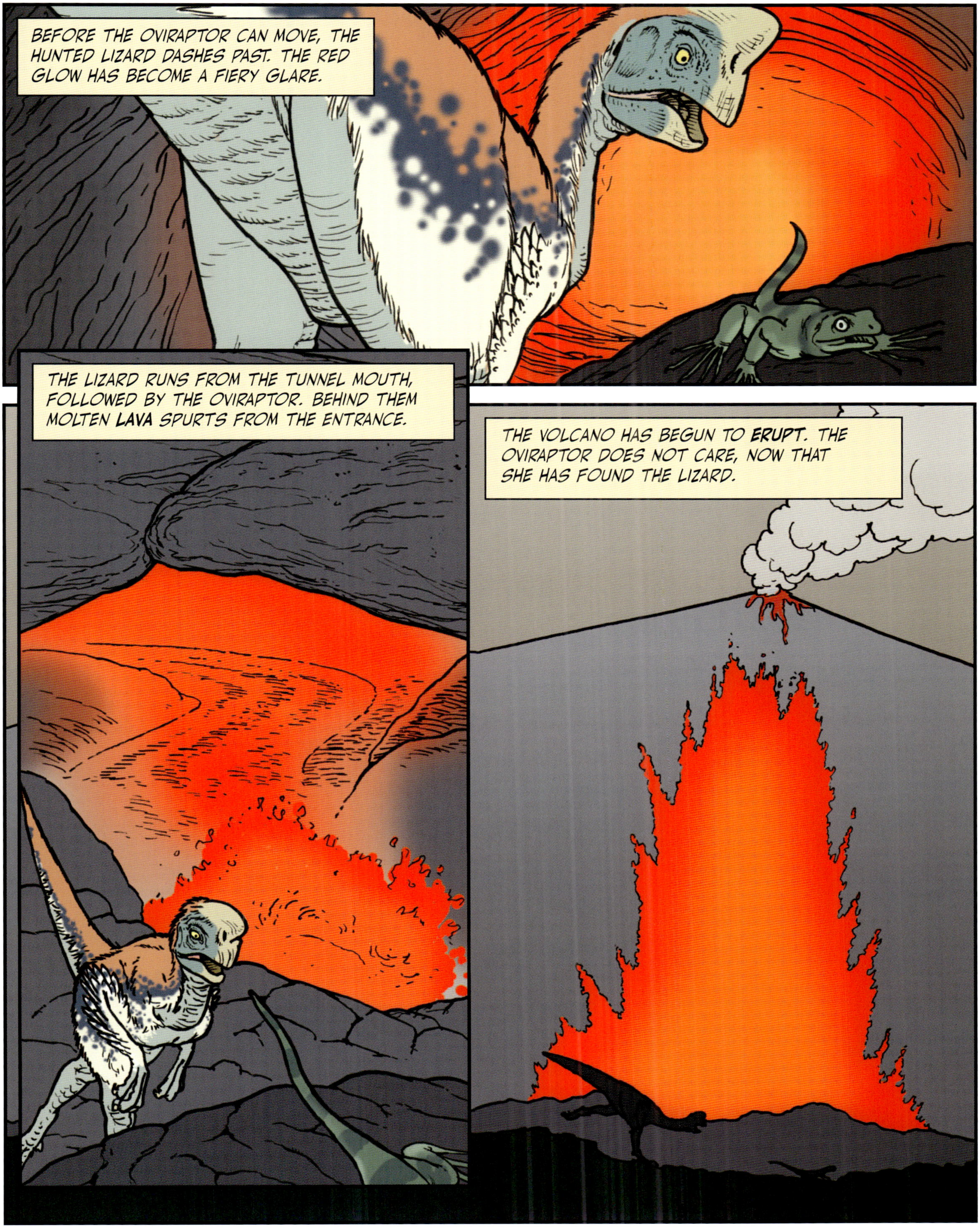
BEFORE THE OVIRAPTOR CAN MOVE, THE HUNTED LIZARD DASHES PAST. THE RED GLOW HAS BECOME A FIERY GLARE.
THE LIZARD RUNS FROM THE TUNNEL MOUTH, FOLLOWED BY THE OVIRAPTOR. BEHIND THEM MOLTEN **LAVA** SPURTS FROM THE ENTRANCE.
THE VOLCANO HAS BEGUN TO **ERUPT**. THE OVIRAPTOR DOES NOT CARE, NOW THAT SHE HAS FOUND THE LIZARD.

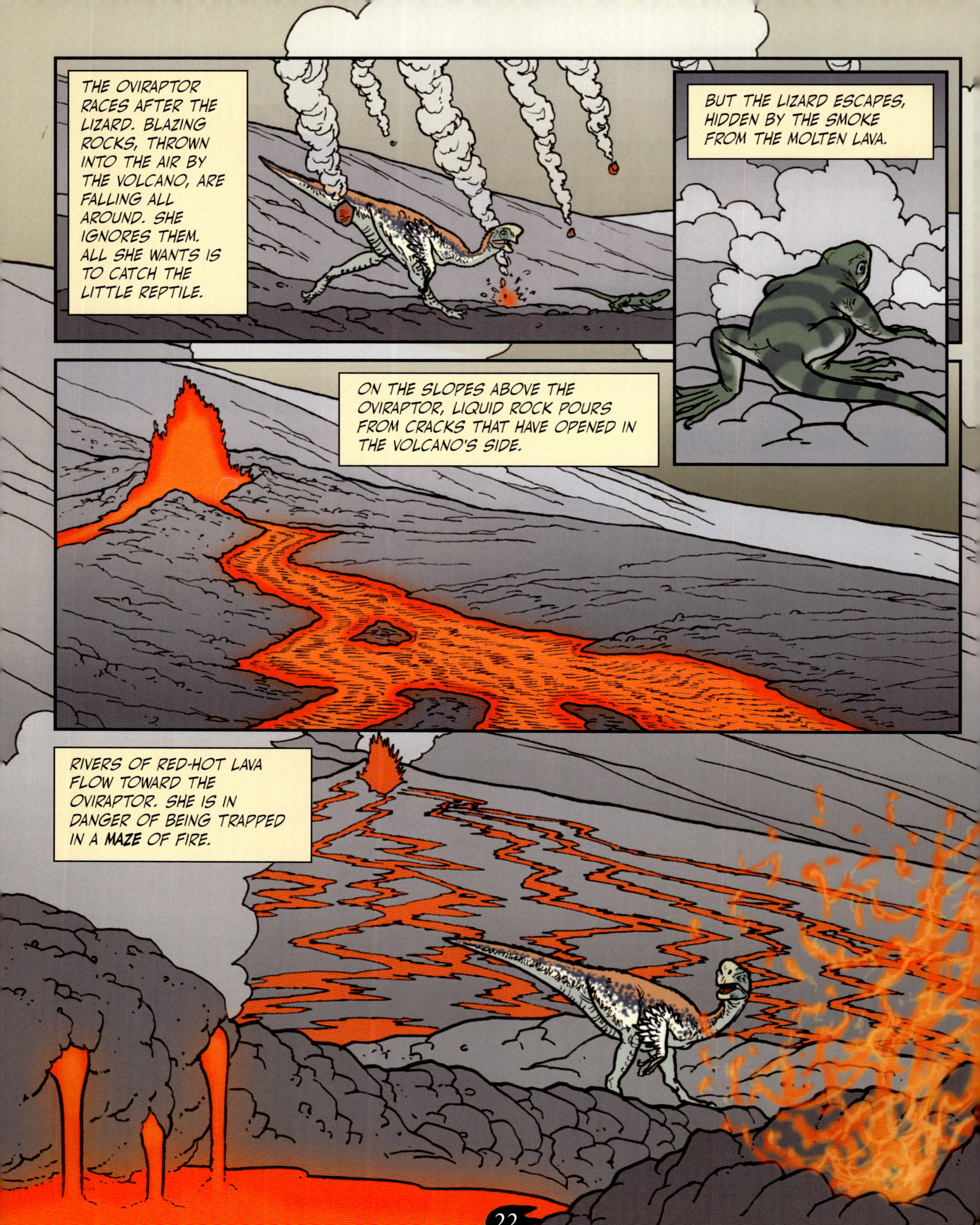
THE OVIRAPTOR RACES AFTER THE LIZARD. BLAZING ROCKS, THROWN INTO THE AIR BY THE VOLCANO, ARE FALLING ALL AROUND. SHE IGNORES THEM. ALL SHE WANTS IS TO CATCH THE LITTLE REPTILE.
BUT THE LIZARD ESCAPES, HIDDEN BY THE SMOKE FROM THE MOLTEN LAVA.
ON THE SLOPES ABOVE THE OVIRAPTOR, LIQUID ROCK POURS FROM CRACKS THAT HAVE OPENED IN THE VOLCANO'S SIDE.
RIVERS OF RED-HOT LAVA FLOW TOWARD THE OVIRAPTOR. SHE IS IN DANGER OF BEING TRAPPED IN A **MAZE** OF FIRE.

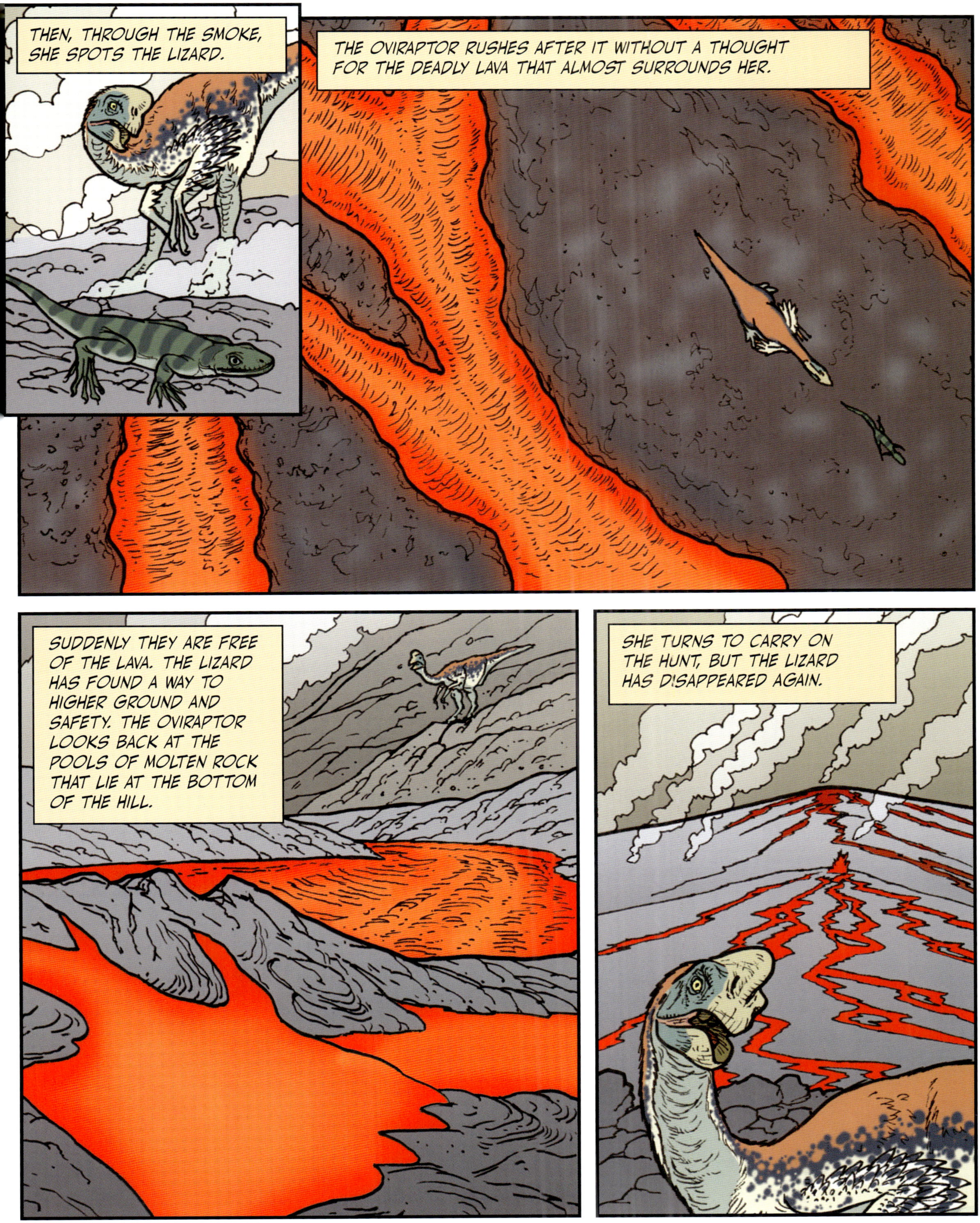
THEN, THROUGH THE SMOKE, SHE SPOTS THE LIZARD.
THE OVIRAPTOR RUSHES AFTER IT WITHOUT A THOUGHT FOR THE DEADLY LAVA THAT ALMOST SURROUNDS HER.
SUDDENLY THEY ARE FREE OF THE LAVA. THE LIZARD HAS FOUND A WAY TO HIGHER GROUND AND SAFETY. THE OVIRAPTOR LOOKS BACK AT THE POOLS OF MOLTEN ROCK THAT LIE AT THE BOTTOM OF THE HILL.
SHE TURNS TO CARRY ON THE HUNT, BUT THE LIZARD HAS DISAPPEARED AGAIN.

PART FOUR... DESERT LIFE

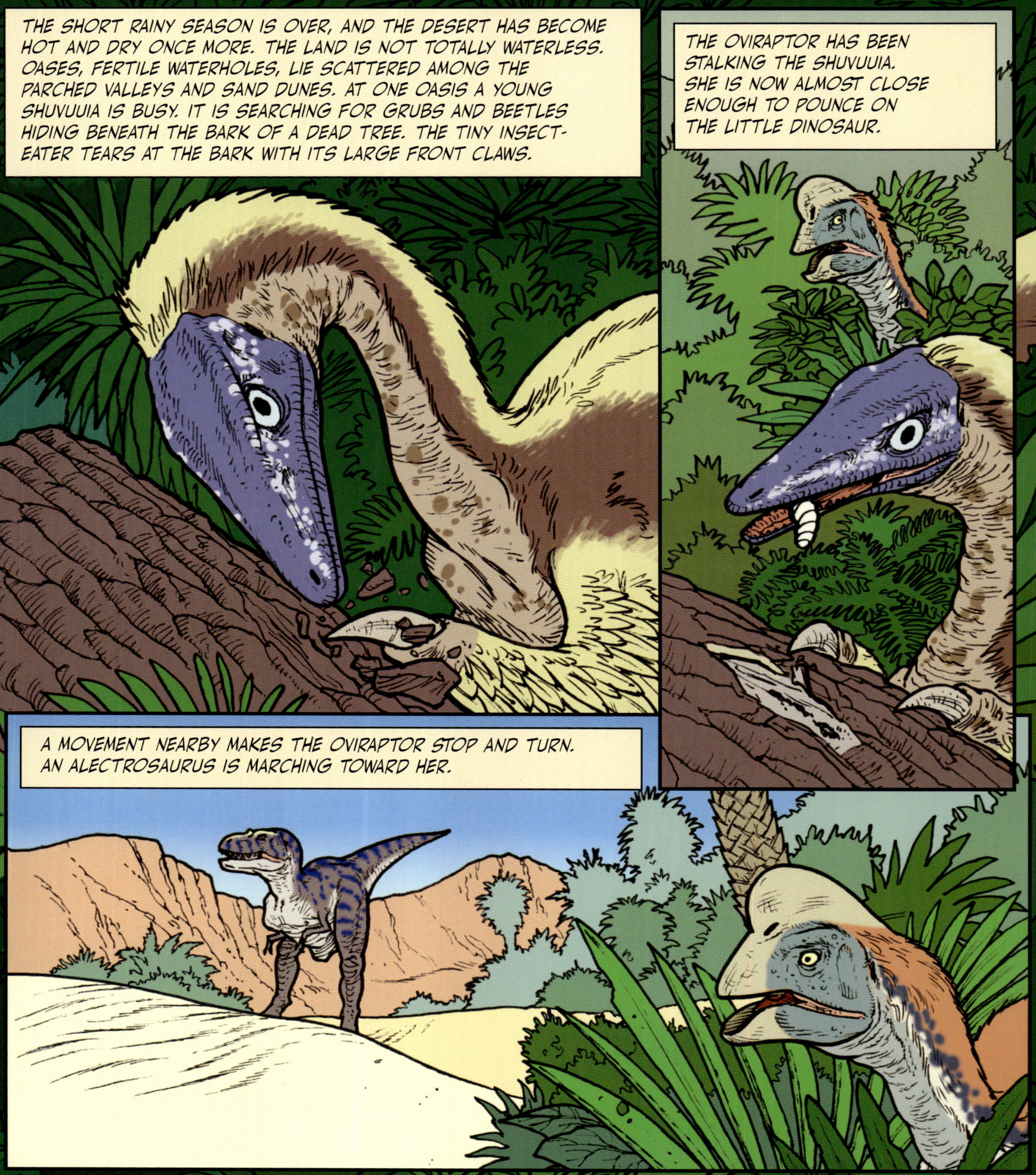

SHE FORGETS ABOUT THE SHUVUUIA AND HIDES.
THE LARGE MEAT EATER IS NOT INTERESTED IN THE OVIRAPTOR.
IT IS HUNTING A HERD OF PROTOCERATOPSES THAT ARE GRAZING AMONG THE DESERT DUNES.
THE OVIRAPTOR FINALLY COMES OUT OF HIDING. THE ALECTROSAURUS HAS GONE, BUT SO HAS THE SHUVUUIA.

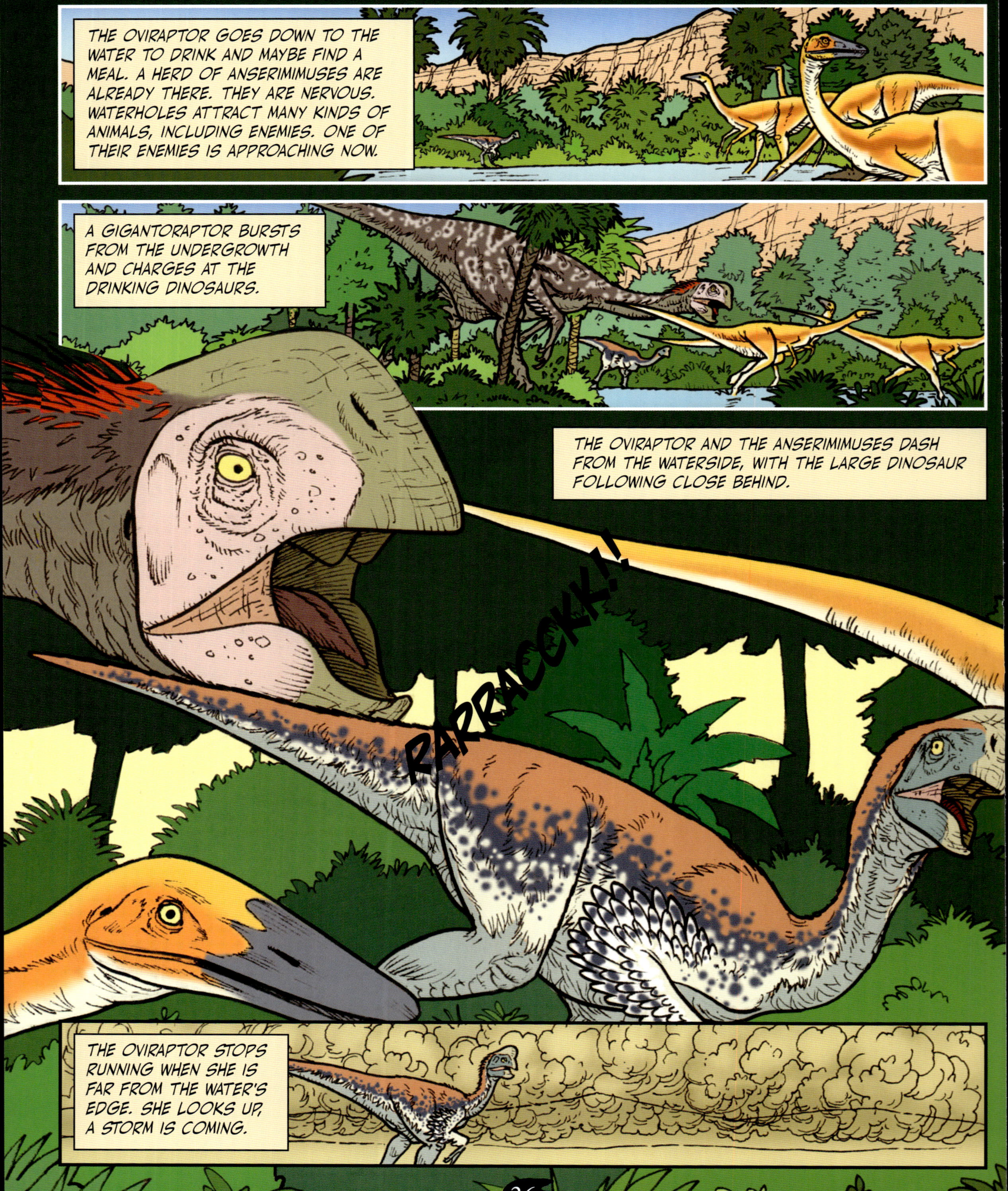
THE OVIRAPTOR GOES DOWN TO THE WATER TO DRINK AND MAYBE FIND A MEAL. A HERD OF ANSERIMIMUSES ARE ALREADY THERE. THEY ARE NERVOUS. WATERHOLES ATTRACT MANY KINDS OF ANIMALS, INCLUDING ENEMIES. ONE OF THEIR ENEMIES IS APPROACHING NOW.
A GIGANTORAPTOR BURSTS FROM THE UNDERGROWTH AND CHARGES AT THE DRINKING DINOSAURS.
THE OVIRAPTOR AND THE ANSERIMIMUSES DASH FROM THE WATERSIDE, WITH THE LARGE DINOSAUR FOLLOWING CLOSE BEHIND.
RARRACCKK!!
THE OVIRAPTOR STOPS RUNNING WHEN SHE IS FAR FROM THE WATER'S EDGE. SHE LOOKS UP, A STORM IS COMING.

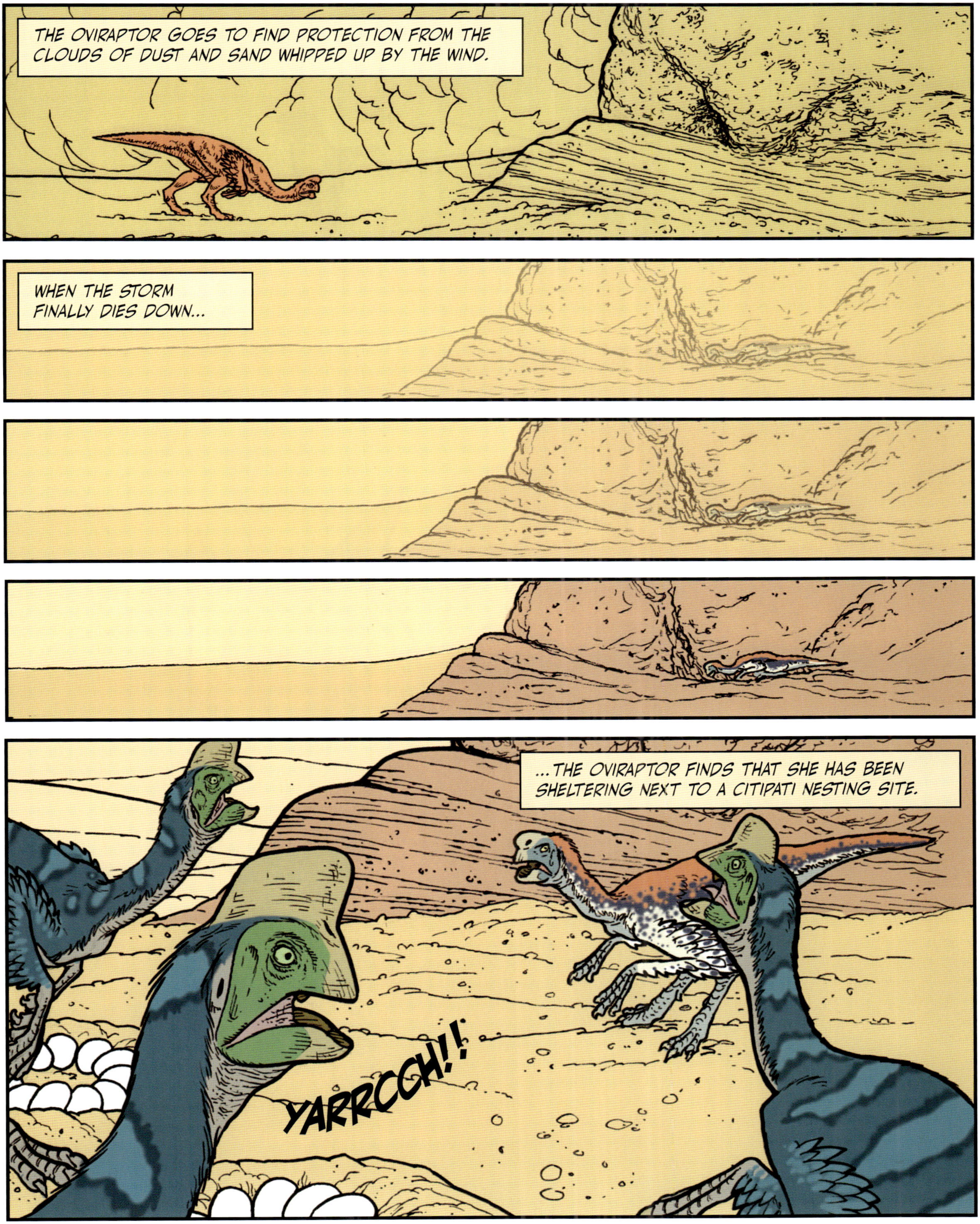
THE OVIRAPTOR GOES TO FIND PROTECTION FROM THE CLOUDS OF DUST AND SAND WHIPPED UP BY THE WIND.
WHEN THE STORM FINALLY DIES DOWN...
...THE OVIRAPTOR FINDS THAT SHE HAS BEEN SHELTERING NEXT TO A CITIPATI NESTING SITE.
YARRCCH!!

THE CITIPATIS THINK THE OVIRAPTOR IS A THREAT TO THEIR EGGS. THEY WILL KILL HER IF THEY CAN CATCH HER.
MEANWHILE, THE ALECTROSAURUS IS STILL HUNTING THE PROTOCERATOPSES. THEY ARE BEING DRIVEN TOWARD THE NESTING SITE.
THE MEAT EATER FINALLY CATCHES A PROTOCERATOPS.
WAARRW!!

THE REST OF THE HERD PANICS AND RUNS.
THE DUNE COLLAPSES UNDER THE WEIGHT OF THE STAMPEDING PROTOCERATOPSES. THE CITIPATIS AND THEIR NESTS ARE BURIED BENEATH A MOUNTAIN OF SAND.
YARRACCKK!!
THE OVIRAPTOR HAS ESCAPED FROM THE TOPPLING DUNE. SHE WALKS AWAY, LEAVING THE BURIED CITIPATIS BEHIND.

FOSSIL EVIDENCE

SCIENTISTS LEARN WHAT DINOSAURS MAY HAVE LOOKED LIKE BY STUDYING THEIR FOSSIL REMAINS. FOSSILS ARE FORMED WHEN THE HARD PARTS OF AN ANIMAL OR PLANT ARE BURIED AND TURN TO ROCK OVER THOUSANDS OF YEARS.

In 1924 American fossil hunter Roy Chapman Andrews led an **expedition** to Mongolia's Gobi Desert. They found the skeleton of a small meat eater. It was lying next to a nest filled with what they thought were the eggs of a dinosaur called Protoceratops. Scientists thought that the dinosaur had died while raiding the nest for its eggs and so it was named "Oviraptor," which means "egg thief."

In the 1990s the fossil of a Citipati, a relative of Oviraptor, was found in Mongolia. It had died sitting on a nest, its arms stretched out to cover the eggs. One of the eggs held the fossil of a Citipati hatchling, proving that the nest belonged to the Citipati. It had been trying to protect its eggs. The eggs were very similar to those lying in the nest found beside the Oviraptor. The little dinosaur had not been stealing Protoceratops eggs after all. The nest was probably its own.

The nest (above) found next to the Oviraptor fossil

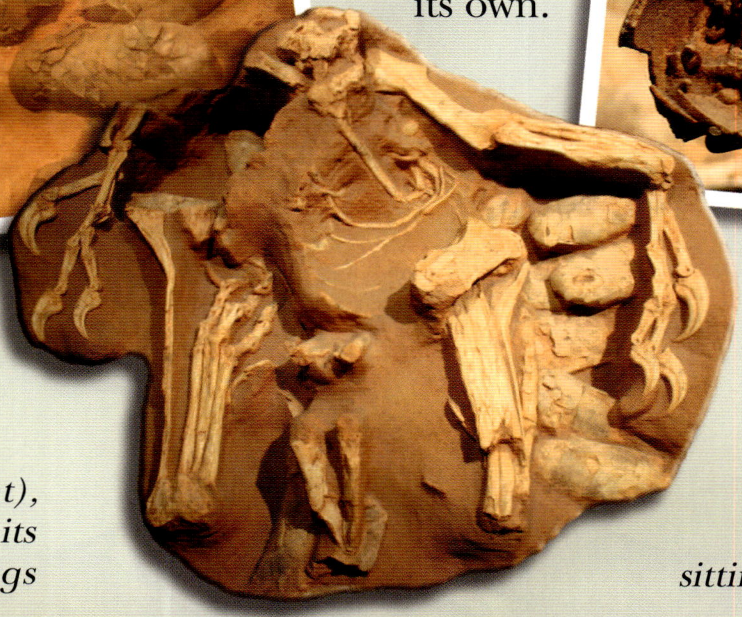

A Citipati fossil (right), showing it sitting on its nest protecting its eggs

A Citipati egg (above), containing a fossilized Citipati hatchling. This proved that the Citipati had been sitting on its own eggs.

ANIMAL GALLERY

ALL THESE ANIMALS APPEAR IN THE STORY.

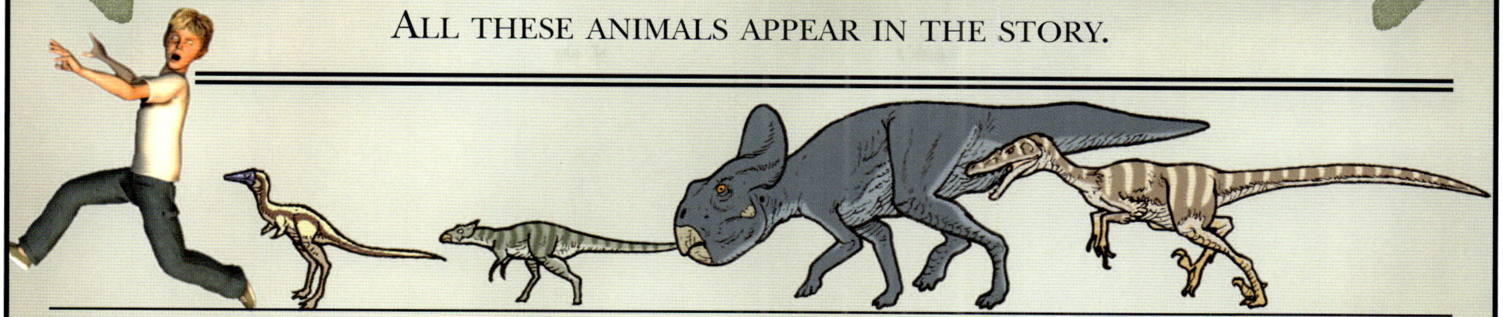

Shuvuuia
"Bird"
Length: 2 ft (60 cm)
A small insect-eating dinosaur that had a powerful digging claw at the end of each arm.

Microceratus
"Small-horned"
Length: 2 ft (60 cm)
A tiny plant eater that walked on two legs and used to be called Microceratops.

Protoceratops
"First horned face"
Length: 6 ft (1.8 m)
A plant eater that lived in herds.

Velociraptor
"Speedy thief"
Length: 6.5 ft (2 m)
A meat-eating dinosaur that may have had feathers.

Citipati
"Funeral pyre lord"
Length: 10 ft (3 m)
A medium-sized Oviraptorid that lived at the same time and place as Oviraptors.

Anserimimus
"Goose mimic"
Length: 14 ft (4 m)
A fast-running omnivore that had powerful arms.

Alectrosaurus
"Unmarried lizard"
Length: 17 ft (5 m)
A medium-sized meat eater that was related to Tyrannosaurus rex.

Tarchia
"Brainy one"
Length: 26 ft (8 m)
A large armored dinosaur that had a bony club on the end of its tail.

Gigantoraptor
"Giant thief"
Length: 26 ft (8 m)
A large, fast-running dinosaur that was a relative of Oviraptor.

Therizinosaurus
"Scythe lizard"
Length: 36 ft (11 m)
A huge plant-eating dinosaur that had 3-foot (0.9 m) long claws.

GLOSSARY

Cretaceous period (krih-TAY-shus PIR-ee-ud) The time between 208 and 146 million years ago.
erupt (ih-RUPT) To eject molten rock and gas from a volcano.
expedition (ek-spuh-DIH-shun) A journey of exploration.
fossils (FO-sulz) The remains of living things that have turned to rock.
lava (LAH-vuh) Molten rock ejected from volcanoes.
maze (MAYZ) A confusing tangle of paths.
parched (PARCHT) Dried out.
prongs (PRONGZ) Thin, pointy pegs.
stalking (STOK-ing) Secretly following someone or something.

INDEX

Web Sites
Due to the changing nature of Internet links, the Rosen Publishing Group, Inc., has developed an online list of Web sites related to the subject of this book. This site is updated regularly. Please use this link to access the list:
www.powerkidslinks.com/gdino/ovirap/